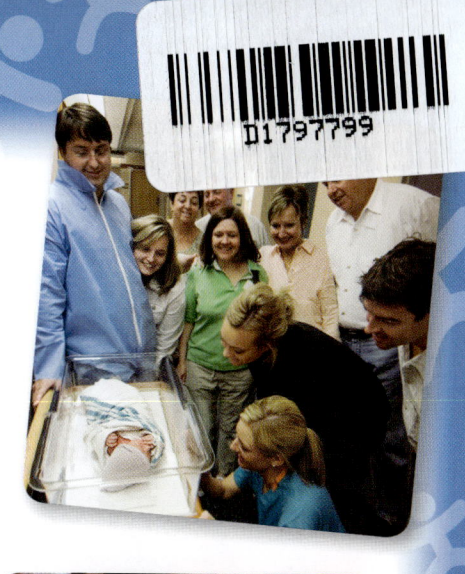

# A New Baby

## New baby, new feelings

 A new baby in the family can make us very happy. But some children have other feelings as well. Can you think why?

Complete the writing for these photos.

1  This girl feels

_____

Maybe she …

_____

2  This boy is

_____

Maybe he …

_____

3  This boy feels

_____

Maybe he …

_____

4  This daddy is

_____

Maybe he …

_____

Learner Profile Attributes: CARING and WELL-BALANCED

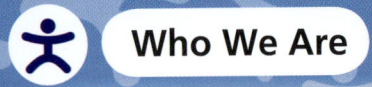 

## Babies grow bigger

For nine months, a baby grows inside its mother.

A photo or drawing of me as a baby.

Sometimes we can see a photo of the baby inside its mother.

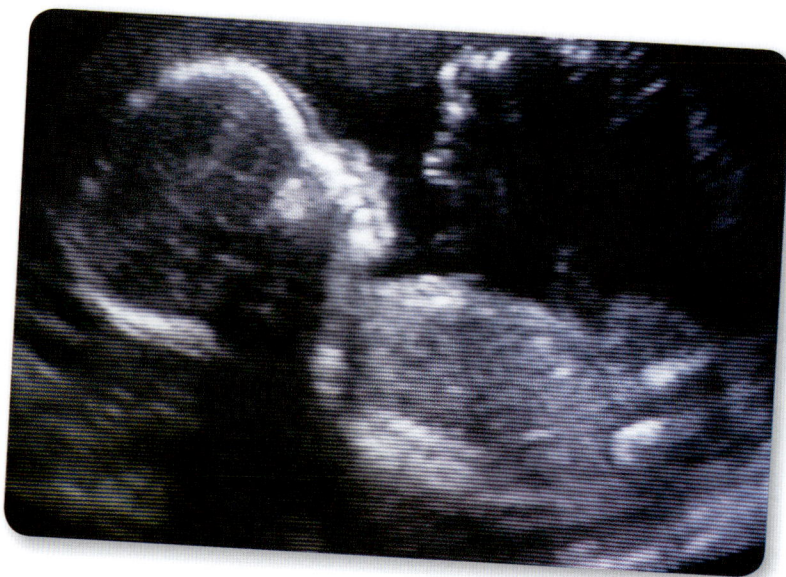

My first word:

_____

When I was born, I weighed:

_____

Now, I weigh:

_____

Learner Profile Attributes: CARING and WELL-BALANCED

## Presents

What would you give a baby?

| Which toy? | Which book? |
|---|---|
| Which pet? | Which idea or promise? Another special gift? |

Complete this poem.

Babies are _____

Babies like _____

Babies say _____

Babies, babies, babies!

Babies go _____

Babies play _____

Babies make _____

Babies, babies, babies!

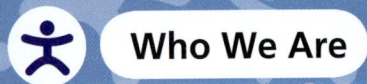 

## Babies need to be safe

Draw circles around all the dangers in this room.

Make a list of things a baby needs.

- _____
- _____
- _____
- _____
- _____
- _____

Now design a room or a bed for a baby.

# What can a baby do?

Write some things a baby can do.

A baby can …

_____

_____

_____

_____

Some families only have one baby. We call this baby an only child. They do not have a brother or sister. What is it like to be an only child? Think about the advantages and disadvantages.

| Advantages | Disadvantages |
|---|---|
|  |  |

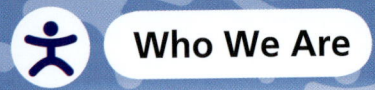 

## Family numbers

Look at this picture of a big family.

How many adults are there?

How many children are there?

Think of some more number questions you could ask about this family.

Here is one:

1   How many toes are there in this family?   Answer: _____

2   _____   Answer: _____

3   _____   Answer: _____

4   _____   Answer: _____

5   _____   Answer: _____

Learner Profile Attributes: CARING and WELL-BALANCED

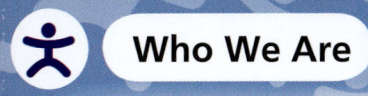 

## Brothers and sisters

 Interview ten friends about their brothers, sisters and cousins. Cousins are the children of your parents' brothers and sisters. Ask: "How many ... do you have?"

| Name of your friend | Number of brothers and stepbrothers | Number of sisters and stepsisters | Number of cousins |
|---|---|---|---|
| | | | |
| | | | |
| | | | |
| | | | |
| | | | |
| | | | |
| | | | |
| | | | |

Now draw a graph on squared paper to show this information.

# Reflection

| Organising theme       | Unit title |
|---|---|
| Write some words you learned in this unit. | |
| Draw or write about something you learned in this unit. | How easy / difficult was this unit?     Write something this unit has helped you do better. |

# Home Sweet Home

## What is a home?

A home is more than just a building. Both of these houses are homes to a family. They are very different, but they are both homes.

| Similarities | Differences |
|---|---|
| | |

Complete the sentences:

Every home needs somewhere to _____

Every home needs somewhere to _____

Every home needs somewhere to _____

Every home needs somewhere to _____

## Homes that move

Draw another home that can be moved.

Some people have homes that they can move!

People who live in houses that move are called _____

I would/would not like to live in this kind of home because _____

_____

## Moving home

Some people move home to live in different places. How many different homes or countries have you lived in? _____

Sometimes we have to leave things behind. But we usually take important or precious things with us when we move. Here is a packing case or crate. If you had to move home what would you pack? Draw and label some important things that you would take with you.

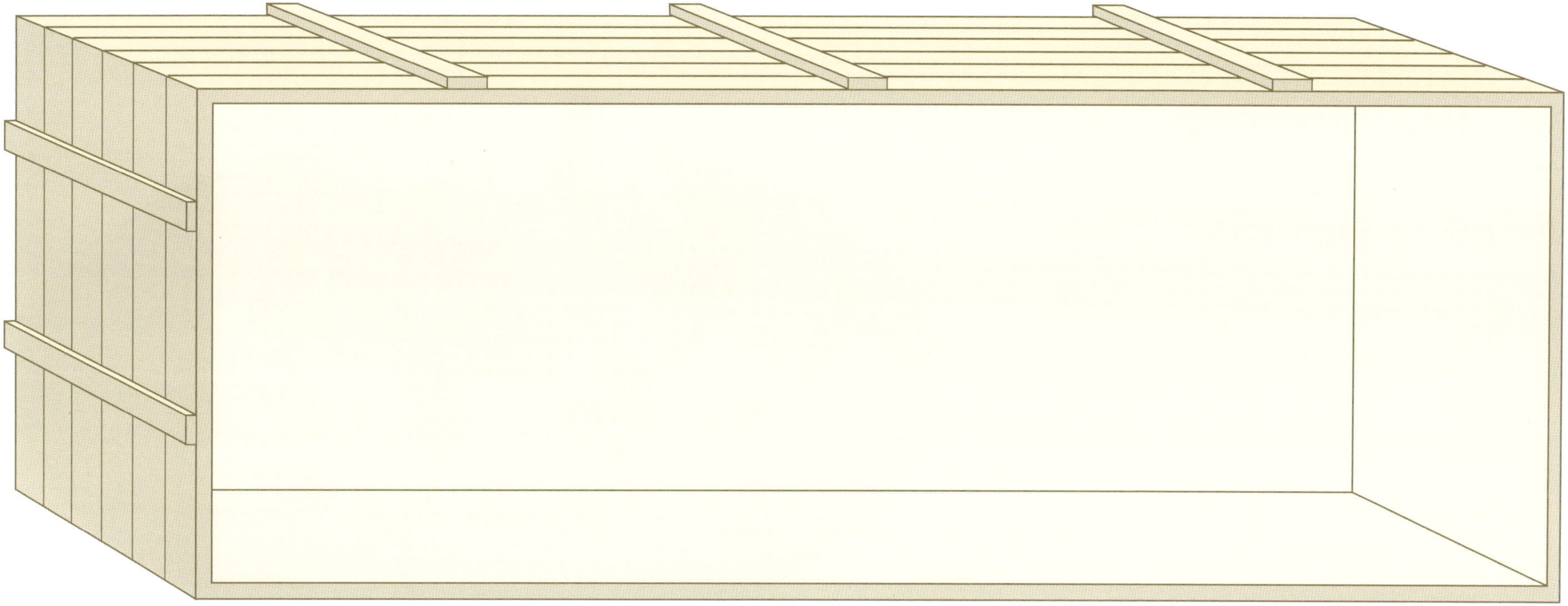

## Walrus and Penguin

Walrus and Penguin are friends. Walrus lives at the North Pole and Penguin lives at the South Pole. They travelled to Egypt to see each other. Trace their journeys on a map or a globe. Which countries did they visit? What did they see?

Penguin went to _____ and _____

He saw _____ and _____

Walrus went to _____ , _____ and _____

He saw _____ , _____ and _____

Now find some other countries they could have visited on their way.

_____

_____

_____

_____

## Think about your home

### What do you like most about it?

_____

_____

_____

_____

_____

_____

### What would you change?

_____

_____

_____

_____

Walrus came to a rain forest in Brazil, where he met a parrot.
"I am too hot," said Walrus.
"I am too hot," said the parrot.
"I miss my nice ice," said Walrus.
"I miss my nice ice," said the parrot.
"Good-bye," said Walrus.
"Good-bye," said the parrot.
Walrus sent a postcard to Penguin.

Dear Penguin,
I am in a hot rain forest with a talking parrot. I wish you were here! I miss my nice ice and I can't wait to see you.
Love,
Walrus

Penguin
South Pole

Walrus misses the ice. What would _you_ miss most about your home if you had to leave it for another one?

_____

_____

_____

_____

## Sharing homes

Some homes have to be shared with other families. In this block of flats, there are hundreds of people living under one roof.

My design for a block of flats

What do you need to think about when you live so close together?

You need to _____

I think living close together could be good because _____

_____

I think living close together could be difficult because _____

Learner Profile Attributes: KNOWLEDGEABLE and OPEN-MINDED

## We all share one home – the Earth

1  Mark your home country on this map of the world in red.

Now draw a map of where you live. Label your road and your home.

2  Add any other places you have called home on the world map in blue.

3  Add any places you have visited on holiday on the world map in green.

# Reflection

| Organising theme       | Unit title |
|---|---|
| Write some words you learned in this unit. | |
| Draw or write about something you learned in this unit. | How easy / difficult was this unit?     Write something this unit has helped you do better. |

# Pictures That Tell Stories

## What do pictures tell us?

Look at this picture. It tells a story about a dragon and two children called George and Georgina.

Tell the story you can see in the picture.

 **Word bank**

castle  dragon  sword  king  queen
prince  horse  princess  twin
fierce  angry  friendly  sad  roar
charge  shake hands  fall down

## Masks

Long ago, people made masks and images of the rain and the wind.

Design a Moon mask to show the face of the Moon, or a Sun mask to show the face of the Sun.

Learner Profile Attributes: COMMUNICATORS and INQUIRERS

## Celtic art

This Celtic bowl seems to tell a story.

Look at it carefully and describe what you see.

_____

_____

_____

Find out three things about the Celts. Write them down.

1 _____

_____

2 _____

_____

3 _____

_____

Design your own bowl

## Egyptian art

 In Ancient Egypt, artists often painted people in profile, from the side. Choose someone you know and draw their profile.

Egyptian picture writing is called hieroglyphics. Write your name in hieroglyphics. Write from top to bottom, downwards.

## A blank vase

The Ancient Greeks and Romans decorated their vases, cups and bowls.

Here is a blank vase.

Draw a fairy tale or another story you know.

Write the outline of the story:

_____

_____

_____

_____

_____

_____

_____

_____

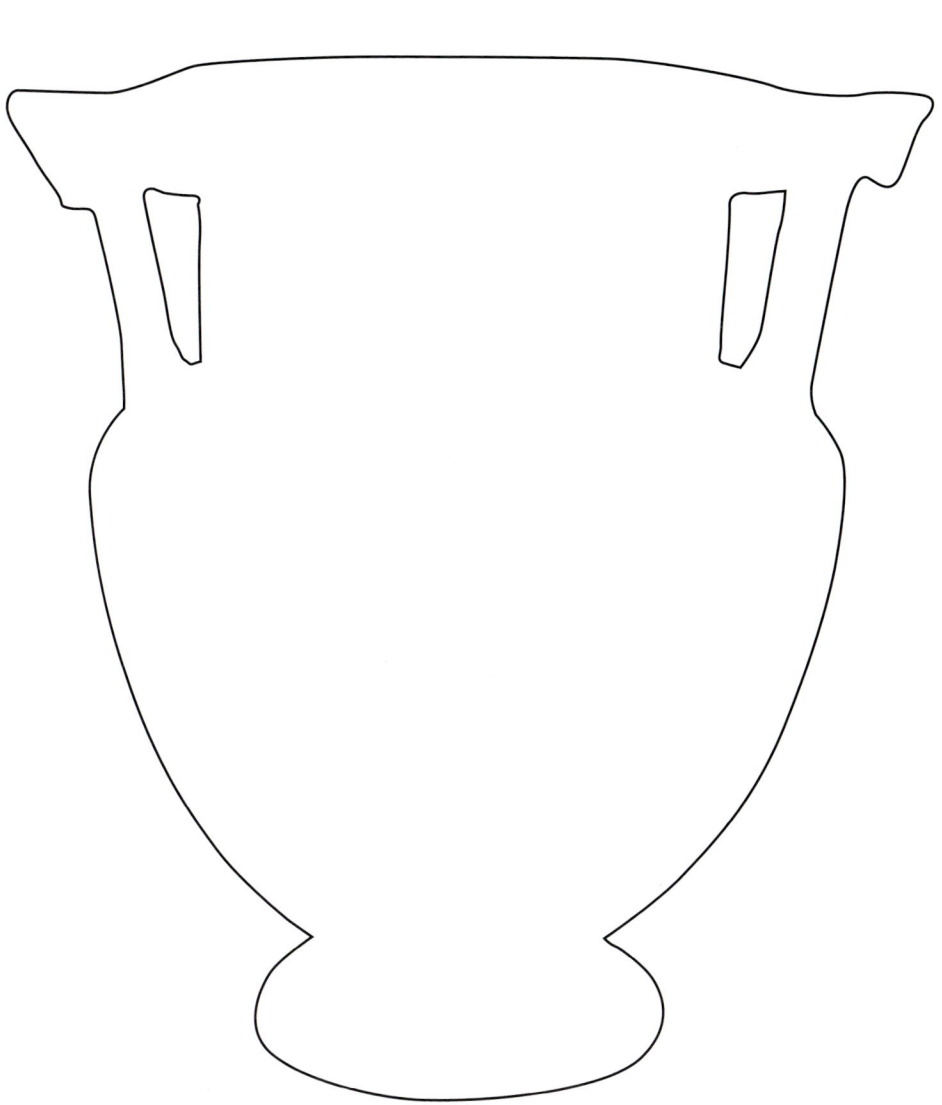

## 📖 Art glossary

Here are some words from the glossary of a book about ancient art.

Match the words to their photos and write the missing definitions.

emperor – A _____

mosaic – ____ _____

mask – ____    a face shape which you can wear

pyramid – ____ _____

sculpture – ____    art which is not flat

hieroglyphics – ____    Egyptian picture writing

temple – ____ _____

tomb – ____ _____

vase – ____    a container for flowers or water

Learner Profile Attributes: COMMUNICATORS and INQUIRERS

## Modern art

Find out about a modern work of art.
Draw it in the box below.

Title: _____

Artist: _____

How is it the same as ancient art?

_____

_____

_____

_____

_____

How is it different?

_____

_____

_____

_____

_____

# Reflection

| Organising theme       | Unit title |
|---|---|
| Write some words you learned in this unit. | |
| Draw or write about something you learned in this unit. | How easy / difficult was this unit?     <br><br> Write something this unit has helped you do better. |

# Discoveries and Inventions

## A timeline of inventions

Here is the timeline of Thomas Edison, a famous American inventor. The timeline shows the main events of his life. They are marked one after another, in sequence.

Mark the five most important events in your life on your own timeline. Draw pictures to illustrate some of them.

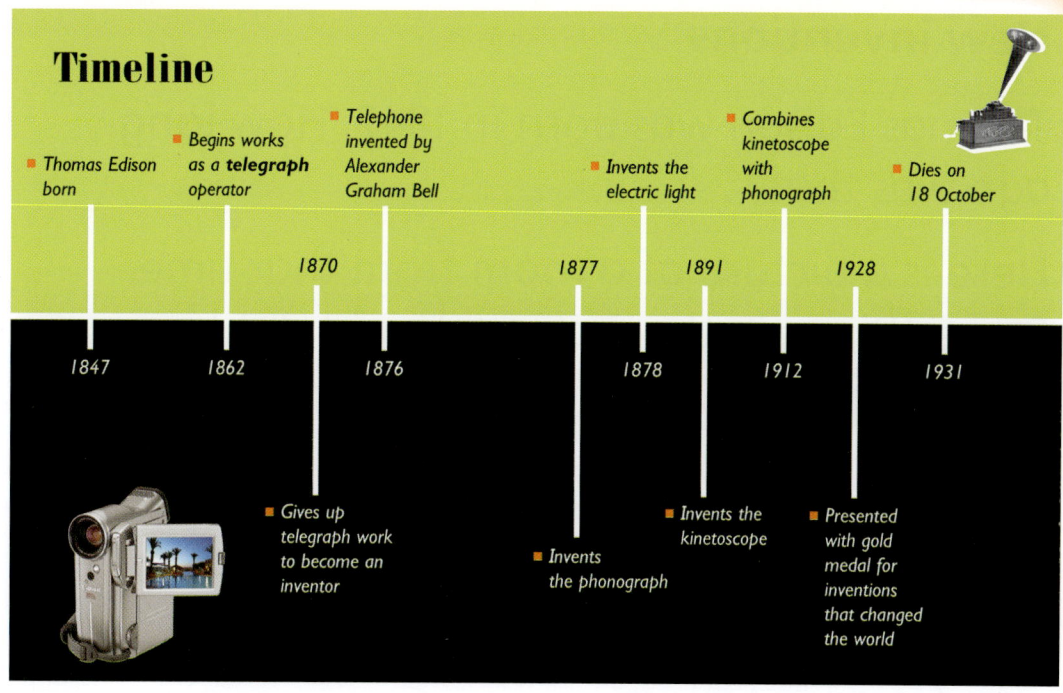

**Timeline**

- Thomas Edison born
- Begins works as a **telegraph** operator
- Telephone invented by Alexander Graham Bell
- Invents the electric light
- Combines kinetoscope with phonograph
- Dies on 18 October

1870    1877    1891    1928

1847    1862    1876    1878    1912    1931

- Gives up telegraph work to become an inventor
- Invents the phonograph
- Invents the kinetoscope
- Presented with gold medal for inventions that changed the world

## New inventions

Thomas Edison was born in 1847. How long ago was that? _____

Here is a picture of a room from that time. Some things in the picture should not be there. They had not been invented! Circle the things that do not belong.

Write a list of the things you circled.

- _____
- _____
- _____
- _____
- _____
- _____

Draw another thing that had not been invented in 1847.

## Three inventions

Thomas Edison's inventions have changed a lot, but we still use his ideas today. Now they are smaller, cheaper and give better sound. They help us to listen and communicate! Find out what you can about these three inventions.

Radio

_____

_____

_____

iPod

_____

_____

_____

Mobile phone

_____

_____

_____

## Light bulbs

Look carefully at a light bulb
(be careful you don't break it!)

Make a sketch of what you see:

Write about how a light bulb works:

_____

_____

_____

_____

There are _____ lights in my classroom.

There are _____ lights in my home.

Draw one of the lights here:

Draw a switch here:

Learner Profile Attributes: THINKERS and KNOWLEDGEABLE

## More inventions

Think about some other things that people have invented to make life easier.

Make a list.

_____

_____

_____

_____

_____

_____

_____

Now choose one and find out more about it.

| What is it? | How does it work? |
|---|---|
| _____ _____ | _____ _____ |
| Who invented it? | Why is it useful? |
| _____ _____ | _____ _____ |
| How has it changed? | Why did you choose it? |
| _____ _____ | _____ _____ |

# Electricity

Some machines use batteries. Others have a plug to use mains electricity. Some machines use both. Find some machines at home. Write their names in the correct spaces in the diagram.

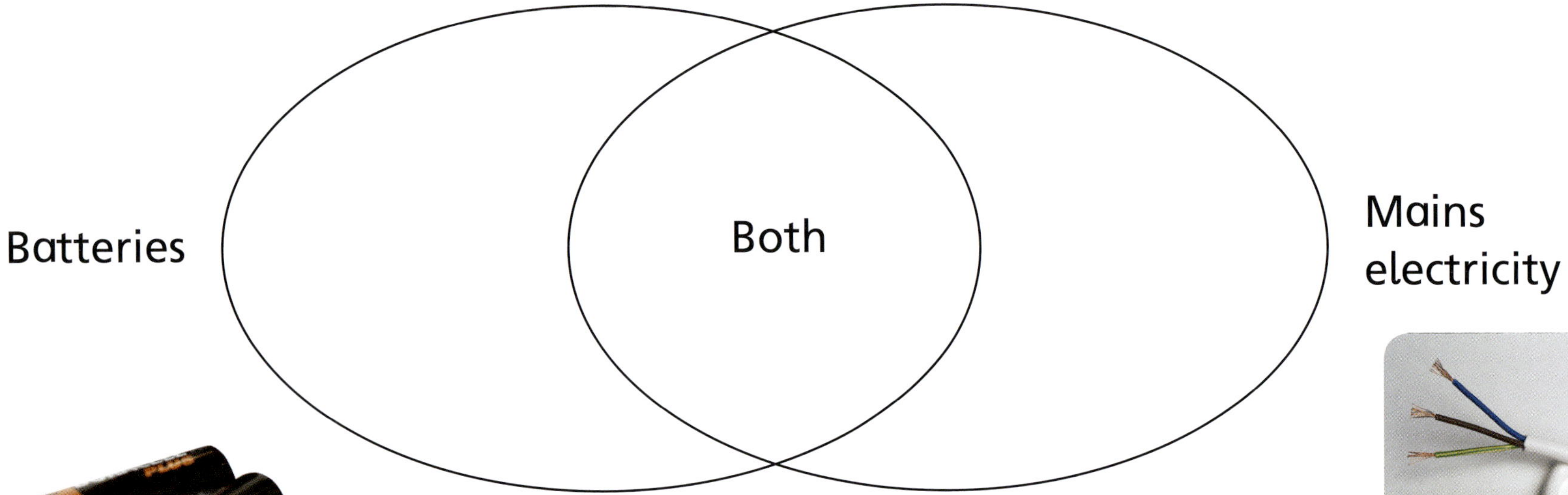

Batteries     Both     Mains electricity

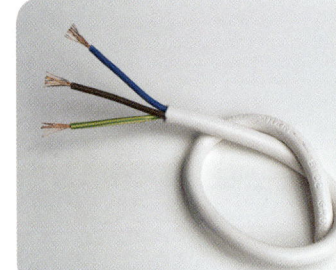

## Machines can be dangerous

Make a safety poster to teach children to be safe.

Invent a machine that can either:

- wake you up in the morning

- weigh a gorilla

- carry an egg safely on wheels

- or do something else …

# Reflection

| Organising theme       | Unit title |
|---|---|
| Write some words you learned in this unit. | |
| Draw or write about something you learned in this unit. | How easy / difficult was this unit?     <br><br> Write something this unit has helped you do better. |

# How Things Are Made

## Where is chocolate made?

Here is a map of the world showing where cocoa and sugar grow.

Cocoa and sugar are used to make chocolate.

Look at the wrapper of your favourite chocolate bar.

Draw the wrapper.

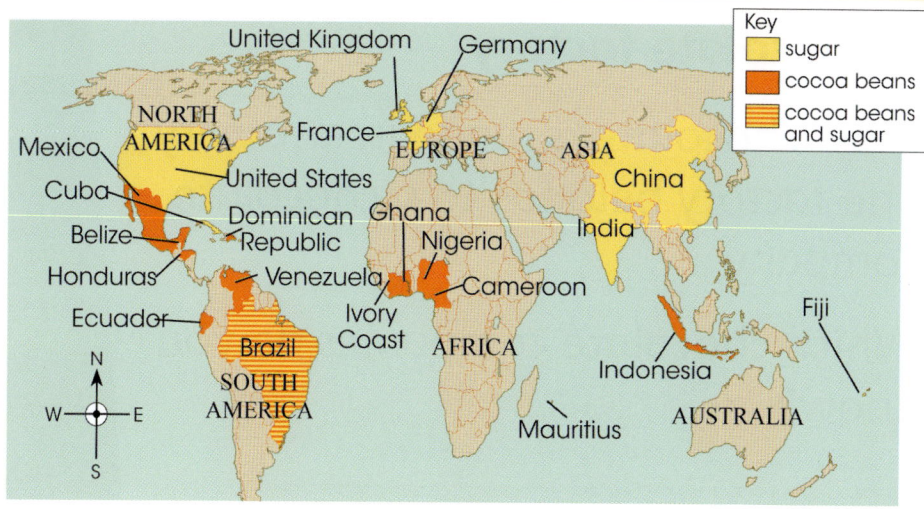

Now write down the ingredients.

_____

_____

_____

How much sugar is there? How much cocoa is there?

_____

_____

_____

## A chocolate factory

Most chocolate is made in a factory. The factory belongs to a chocolate company.

Which chocolate companies do you know?

_____

_____

_____

Inside a chocolate factory, there are lots of machines and a few people. Write down what you can you see in this picture.

_____

_____

_____

_____

Learner Profile Attributes: PRINCIPLED and REFLECTIVE

## From cocoa to chocolate

Chocolate bars are made from cocoa pods.

Draw or describe the four main stages of making chocolate.

| 1 | 2 |
|---|---|
| 3 | 4 |

## Keeping clean

It is very important that the chocolate factory is kept clean.

What can the people who work there do to keep everything clean?

_____

_____

_____

_____

_____

_____

_____

_____

_____

_____

Learner Profile Attributes: PRINCIPLED and REFLECTIVE

# A chocolate shop

How does chocolate reach the shops?

_____

_____

_____

Look at this display of chocolate bars.

Make up a different price for each bar. Write them in the circles. Then complete the table below.

| Chocolate name | Number of bars | Price per bar | Total |
|---|---|---|---|
| Crunch | 2 | | |
| Yum Yum | 1 | | |
| Choco Loops | 3 | | |
| Button Chocs | 2 | | |
| Choc Fun | 1 | | |

Add up the price of all the bars. How much money will the shopkeeper take if he adds up all the totals?

Grand total =

## Fair Trade

What does this symbol mean? _____

Where have you seen it? _____

What does it show? _____

Why is it helpful to cocoa and sugar farmers?

_____

Draw a Fairtrade farmer on his/her farm:

What is he/she growing?

_____

_____

_____

_____

Find out more about Fairtrade and Max Havelaar.

_____

_____

Learner Profile Attributes: PRINCIPLED and REFLECTIVE

## Word puzzles

Write as many words as you can, using some of the letters in the word 'chocolate'.

_____

_____

_____

Tick the things that start with 'ch'. Circle the one that ends with 'ch'.

# Reflection

| Organising theme       | Unit title |
|---|---|
| **Write some words you learned in this unit.** | |
| **Draw or write about something you learned in this unit.** | **How easy / difficult was this unit?**     **Write something this unit has helped you do better.** |

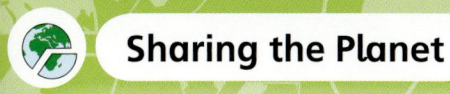

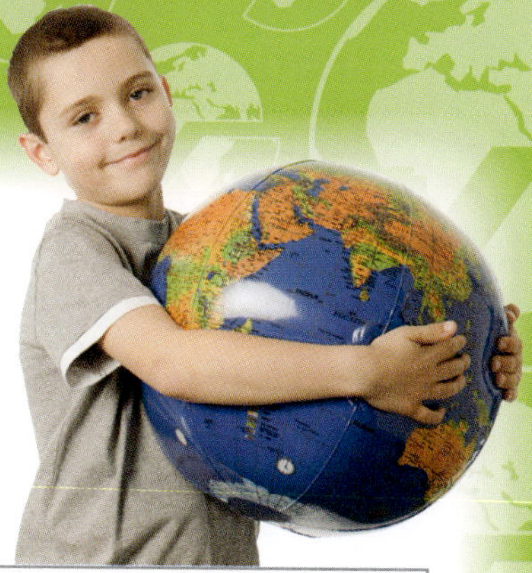

# Planet in Danger

## What are the problems?

Draw and write about three problems that face our planet, Earth.

Learner Profile Attributes: PRINCIPLED and RISK-TAKERS

## Pollution

What is pollution?

_____

What can we do about pollution?

_____

Look at these ideas. Tick the ones you already do.

- ○ recycle glass, plastic and metal
- ○ re-use old things
- ○ cut back on rubbish
- ○ clean up litter
- ○ walk or cycle to school
- ○ take part in a car share scheme
- ○ take a bus or a train instead of the car
- ○ use environmentally-friendly cleaning products
- ○ use a shopping basket instead of plastic bags

Learner Profile Attributes: PRINCIPLED and RISK-TAKERS

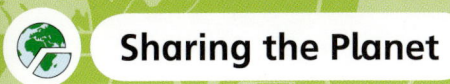 

## Trees

Write as many tree words in the branches as you can.

## What can we do to protect trees?

_____

_____

_____

_____

_____

_____

_____

_____

_____

_____

_____

_____

# What a lot of rubbish!

How much does a wastepaper basket of rubbish weigh? _____

This girl is helping her father to take out the rubbish.

They collect rubbish in plastic bags. How much do you think a bag full of rubbish weighs? _____

In the UK, a family can throw away I tonne of rubbish per year. What is a tonne? _____

How many tonnes does an elephant weigh? _____

How many tonnes does a blue whale weigh? _____

How many tonnes does your family car weigh? _____

Learner Profile Attributes: PRINCIPLED and RISK-TAKERS

## Leaves

Collect some leaves. Look at them through a magnifying glass.

Find out how a leaf works. How does it breathe? Draw a diagram or picture to explain it.

Now design a wild area or garden for your school.

Now draw three different leaf shapes.

Find out which trees they come from.

## Saving the rainforests

If we don't protect our rainforests, they will disappear in less than 50 years. How old will you be then? _____ Maybe we still have time to save the rainforests. What can we do?

We can _____

_____

_____

Who could you write to, with your ideas?

_____

_____

_____

Write a letter to one of these organisations or people. Draft it here.

Learner Profile Attributes: PRINCIPLED and RISK-TAKERS

# Animals in the rainforest

Draw some of the endangered animals that live in the rainforest.

# Reflection

| Organising theme       | Unit title |
|---|---|
| Write some words you learned in this unit. | |

| Draw or write about something you learned in this unit. | How easy / difficult was this unit?<br><br>   <br><br>Write something this unit has helped you do better. |